# Poetry from a Thoughtful Mind

## By George Howard

This is my second book in a series of poetry compilations, a sequel to 'Poetry from a Tangled mind'. It is another collection of various poems, using themes drawn from mine, and close friends' personal events, and also the world in general. Some are fiction, many based on fact, but again they are all from the heart.

I would once more like to thank all of my friends, for their continued support, and to my good friend and writing buddy Mark Bradshaw, an exceptional writing talent. Thanks for your critique and gentle pushes in the right direction mate.

Mark runs a small but beautiful site for all budding wannabees, free and friendly; http://blog4free.ning.com



ISBN: 978-1-4467-7672-8

## Contents

## Spring Forth

The sun, once more awakening dawn choristers.
Songbirds, sweet music, to make the genius composer weep.
Strolling once more down lanes, sentries of Hawthorn and Privet.
Now in uniforms new, garbs in shades of emerald.
Lawns and pavements once more covered white,
Carpeted with petal confetti, leaving cherries blushing, naked, behind,
Blades of lush new green, pushing defiantly forth with jubilance,
To greet the newly awakening world, of birth and growth.
Humming workers, dressed in black and yellow sweaters,
Tireless and urgent, one track minded unselfish wonders.
Unwittingly, spreading procreation, and thus joy to all,
Blossoms of incalculable variations of hues, colouring hedgerows,
Fields and gardens, sweet scents, aromas fit for Gods.
Babbling brooks, tumbling into limpid pools, teeming with life renewed,
Gondolas of white lilies, hosting croaking Gondoliers.
Lambs pulled swiftly into a glittering world,
Milking stool gait, unsteady and unsure.
Startled woolly creatures with drunken stagger,
Morphing next, into bleating, galloping joy.
Male feathered dinosaurs, strutting, and boasting their finery.
Females averting, glancing sideways, looking for perfect form.
Taking to the wing, playing the game of love and survival.
Males follow on, feeling the urgency of proliferation.
Warm sunny days, easing joints and lightening hearts.
Dreams of lazy days to come, of lemonade fizz,
Of strawberries red and candy coloured skirts.
Would it were that these days never ending be.

## A Part Time Position

I stand at the bar; it's a part time position.
Thought over carefully, not a spur of the moment decision.
It was either this, or sit down with the wife for a talk.
I told her instead, I would take the dog for a walk.
I stand at the bar; it's a part time position.
When I said, "Back in one hour!" She'd stared with derision.
But I'll show her, I will, I'll show her who's strong.
I'll stick to two pints and prove to her, she's wrong!
I stand at the bar; it's a part time position.
I'll stick to my plans; I don't want any fuss, or kind of collision.
I've been fifty minutes now, I can squeeze in another.
If it takes a little longer, say five minutes! I can cover.
I stand at the bar; it's a part time position.
If she asks how many pints I've had, she's getting no admission.
Who does she think she is my boss, or my keeper?
May as well have another, after five it gets cheaper!
I stand at the bar; it's a part time position.
May as well have another couple, as I'm definitely heading for perdition.
I'll swear that the dog ran off and was a bitch to find.
Now if I can just get my story right, try to keep it in mind!
I stand at the bar; it's a part time position.
As I blamed the dog, she stared, then said it was of my own volition.
I struggled upstairs in the dark and the gloom.
She slammed our door, so I was confined to the spare room.
I stand at the bar, it's a permanent position.
As today, my wife left me high and dry, ran away with the electrician!
Still! It's not so bad, I think, as I 'pop another cork'.
At least I don't anymore, have to take the dog for a walk!

## A Perfect Form

I stopped and stooped the other day,
I don't know why, I'm sorry I just can't say!
I held a daisy in my hand; it looked so small and fragile,
And then, as if not seen before, it did beguile
Me with its beauty. As I looked and did behold,
Perfect form and symmetry coloured white and gold.
I held it for an age and could not let go.
Its wonderment filled my soul, flooding me so,
With tears. I just cannot explain the joys I felt,
I beheld its wondrous beauty, as I dwelt,
This perfect almost secret form, unseen by the daily eye.
Given not a second thought, as humans passed it by.
Please take advice, if you would, you will prosper, tarry a while.
Cup carefully your hand, around bloom and leaf, believe, you will smile,
Or shed a tear or two.

## Mates to the End

Jimmy sat on 'his' public bench, a smile on his face.
The sun shone down now, of the cold, no longer a trace.
The *faces* passed by, some taking him in, some full of scorn.
Many passing judgement, without knowing, a few torn,
Between pity and derision, none understanding, his torment and pain.
Jimmy glanced around, an agitated look on his face, in strain.
Wherever was Malcolm? He was never this late.
Malcolm was his best friend, his bosom buddy, his mate.
They'd been together just yesterday, drinking away the gloom.
Jimmy had said goodbye, outside his flat and staggered to his room.
His anxiety was growing now, Malcolm was seldom on time.
But to be as delayed as this, didn't make reason nor rhyme.
He paced up and down, now really getting in a mess.
Chewing at his fingernails, and filling up with stress.
Then suddenly Jimmy spotted Malcolm's face through the crowd.
All the tension flooded away, he was so grateful, he almost bowed
To his knees, in prayer, "Thank you God up on high!"
Instead he let out a yell of laughter, and ended with a sigh.
"Hi mate!" He cried "You're late, where have you been?"
Malcolm looked at him puzzled, "No sweat man, I was just feeling green!"
They hugged each other, cajoling and thumping with glee.
Caring not about the *faces*, not concerned whether they would see.
They broke open the 'champagne', which Jimmy had brought.
Their 'Elixir of Life', passed from lip to lip, numbing senses, as sought.
Their main aim now to 'dumb out' the cruel senseless world all around,
So they may speak, without interruption, of things important and profound.
They jabbered about nothing, putting their own personal world to rights;
The price of Cider, the Community Patrollers, last night's arguments and
fights.

They never watch the TV, neither to the radio do they listen.
No concern for Tsunamis, or volcanoes, nor if a new Messiah has risen.
All they need worry about are their meagre funds at present,
Whether to get more Cider, or buy some food, which they resent.
They plump for the cider, "Get the cheapest you can, three bottles, don't forget!"
Off shuffles Malcolm, on his daily chore, checks out shops, for the cheapest one yet.
Jimmy now feeling conscious, of the state he is in, looks down at his feet.
"Those trainers need replacing", he'll cadge some tomorrow, beg in the street
And into a Charity shop, looking for the cheapest he can possibly buy,
Pointless wasting money, in fact sometimes he can blag them, if he really does try.
The lovely women in the shops understand, and will try and help out.
They won't give him money, but they don't make a fuss or shout.
"There but for the grace…" He often hears them remark.
They know what life is about, that the reality is stark.
It ain't no bed of roses, you don't get a hand up the ladder.
You very rarely get a friendly handshake, which is so much sadder.
Jimmy sees Malcolm returning, loaded up with 'promise'.
"Sorry I was so long mate I was hearing about Old Doris!"
Old Doris had a trolley, and she shoved it around town.
Apparently well off at one time, but then, life had got her down,
Into the gutter, collecting odds and ends, nothing of value, to be seen.
Some say she still had money, "Nearly as much as a Queen!"
Just hadn't the sense now to claim it, and didn't really care.
Would go to the Park bench she loved, and just sit and stare
At the children and mothers who played there on hot summer days.
She would watch a while and chuckle, saying "They never cease to amaze!"
Doris hadn't married, had looked after her parents all of her life.
They had been sick, she, no time for men, alone, no chance to be a wife.
An only child, left all the money and the house, in the will.
Life had passed her by, and often the tears fell still.
But no longer, for Doris, who had been found in a heap,
Two minutes from her house, apparently she just fell asleep.
She hadn't awoken, carried on to her journeys end, it did seem.

Her pain no more, now left to the police and a forensic team.
Jimmy and Malcolm hit the bottle in earnest, no lunch nor tea.
Downing the cheap cider, so much, they could hardly see.
Laughing and chattering in their usual slurry chat,
Sporting glazed expressions, Jimmy grinning like a Cheshire cat,
At everyone who passed by, not seeing the looks of disgust.
Malcolm saying "Count up, have we enough for another? Only just!"
Off he goes, to the shop once more, leaving Jimmy alone,
Who tries to stand, falls over, hits his head, down like a stone.
As Malcolm comes back, he sees the blue flashing light,
"What's happened now, something to make his life bright?"
He stares in disbelief when he sees his best pal prone,
On the pavement, blood running free, letting out a moan.
"Jimmy! You okay mate?" he shouts already confused.
His pal carried off on a stretcher, as he stands in shock, bemused.
Malcolm plucks up the courage after two bottles of grog,
His shakes now subsiding, mind now in a hazy fog.
He calls at the hospital reception, pretty girl on the counter.
Malcolm thinking, "I'll ask her, she'll know, she's bound to".
Pretty girl says, "Jimmy who please sir, are you a relation?"
He stood in a panic, motionless in confused hesitation.
"Er.. I'm afraid I don't know that, I've forgotten his name"
He stood there alone, frightened and in abject shame.
"He's a 'street' guy, my buddy, my friend. You know what I mean!"
"Just take a seat over there Sir, I'll see if you can be seen!"
Malcolm sat in the corner away from them all.
Slipping into withdrawal, when all of a sudden, a call.
"Malcolm Smith please!" It seemed strange hearing his name.
Standing up too quickly, tripping over, "The chair was to blame!"
"Come this way please Sir" said the doctor, taking his arm.
"I've some very bad news!" Malcolm now stared in alarm.
He, now all of a sudden sober, after a long time in his life.
His blood now racing, adrenalin rush, head already full of strife.
He ran out as fast as he could, not wanting to hear more.
Running as far as he could until his muscles were sore.
Malcolm sat down and wept for his loss and his pain.
Never would he drink with his best buddy Jimmy again.
He was weeping for himself as well as for his friend.

What would he do with his life now? On him he did depend.
Malcolm sat on 'his' public bench, a smile on his face,
Wherever was Pete? Probably still drunk back at his place!
If he didn't turn up soon, he would give him the sack!
Malcolm suddenly winced, put his hand on the awful pain, in his lower back.

## Memories Residing

Oh to lay me down in fields of golden wheat prostrate,
Watching cotton clouds cross azure blue skies and abate.
Helios gazing down, warming me with tender, gentle care.
Hawk on high, stalling and climbing, but ever watchful stare.
Stone like decent, silent and deadly end to tiny mouse or shrew.
To see old man beetle, dashing by, rushing where, if only he knew.
Sitting upon rocks, as squabbling water tumbles by, o'er pebble gems.
Flowing forth, with excitement and glee, down hills and glens.
Clean and crisp babbling stream, proffering cheek, for icy kiss.
Pure, newborn anew, promise of life, giving succour and earth bliss.
Seeing a miracle, a birth, a lamb, a completion of cyclic life,
Gambolling gangly fools, celebrating, no fear of the butcher's knife.
Walking velvet, newly mown meadow, ambrosia rivalled by few.
Carpets of purple-blue velvet and gold, labouring with dew.
Aromas flooding senses, as blooms and herbs compete to win favours.
Insects, called, obey, enraptured by delicious, scented flavours.
The earthy odours of fresh turned soil, gently stinging nostrils wide.
Chastising Seagulls, flocking to the plough and forgetting the tide.
Bushes of Blackbirds warbling chorus, sharp, true and bright.
The Judas Cuckoo, trying to compete, as the Skylark takes flight,
High aloft to heaven she climbs, all but out of sight, a fluttering speck.
To out-fox the Fox, the Weasel and Stoat, her clutch unguarded upon the deck.

She sings her song of deft deceit, completing distraction, a clever tool.
Then danger past, she floats down, several yards adrift, again to fool.
She zig-zags, towards the nest, where waits her mate, the last defence.
The fox trots by, the ruse worked, he'd seen the bird, knew not whence.
Dusk veiled hedgerows, silhouettes of black against a Shepherd's sky, render.
Orange grove clouds, tearing the even skies asunder, with resultant vista splendour.
Gnats dance like fools, with gay abandon, swirling around a wafted hand.
Grasshoppers, rubbing legs on wings, Nightjars join chorus, for the evening's band.
I lay my head on downy pillow, watching through open window now,
Awaiting Morpheus, drinking in the night, and all the day did bestow.

## A Chronological Mistake

Epochs tumble into the hedgerows of time,
Leaving me grasping memories of a love sublime.
Friendships true as Eros' arrows, timeless bonds.
Life's pages, full of Truffle moments, and regretted wrongs.
Processions of Trojan visitors, with Judas intentions,
Venus visiting, sometimes unwanted affections.But all bringing their own hue, to succour an overflowing pot.
Leaving me oft times, a cacophony, to spoil my lot,
My life's symphony, my biography, an existence so futile
It seems, at times wondering, "what's worthwhile?"
Then other times so wonderful, my heart may break,
It's fragile form, beating so hard, no more could it take.
A moment of this journey I would never change, true.
But my love, to have again an hour with you,
I would gladly surrender the rest of my time,
For I know this encounter would be so sublime.

## The Time Is Near

When I look at all the hurt and anger in the world. I sometimes despair.
All the lies and deceit, in the name of religion and injustice, which
becomes unjust
itself.
Evil is as a red hot poker, you can see it, sometimes you can feel it near,
you are
not able to grasp it!
Love is a fluid thing, it flows from person to person, like a river, it will
gather
momentum.
Until at the very end a calm gentle flow remains
As with water, grip your hands tightly, try to keep it for yourself, nothing
but drops
remain.
Hold it gently and let it trickle out, you will always be left with plenty.
We must all learn to love and accept love, for if we do not we will be lost
forever.
The time is oh so much closer than we realise

## Fun In the City

Passing doors of torturous din,
Glancing through at the sheep within.
Competing Bulls, testosterone soaked air.
Spangled females, skirts short, legs bare.
Talking the talk of fools, laced with shot after shot.
Boasting idiots, lying about drinks they'd had, not.
Legless Jesters, kissing the gutters, unable to rise.
Girlfriends stooping to lift them, unable, with surprise,
Beckoning colleagues to help, with their chore.

Penguin bouncers looking on and laughing, on the door.
They've seen it so many times, never ceases to amaze.
Watching all the drunken hordes staggering in a haze.
Round and round in circles they go.
Following the 'action', going with the flow.
Next, it's off to the nightclubs, queuing for miles.
Looking like frightened cattle, locked up in stiles.
Fooling the doormen, giving false identity,
Popping pills, trying to fool and prove their sobriety.
Bragging sops at the bar, "Give us alcohol, we'll sup it!"
Falling about the dance floor, like a string-less puppet.
Thrown out to the taxi ranks, retching up over a fence.
Jumping the queue, a signal for fighting to commence.
Ten onto one, he just doesn't stand a chance.
No one to help him, not one dare advance.
He tries running the gauntlet, just makes twenty feet.
The pack hits and trips him, he crashes to the floor, now beat.
But they don't stop now, for blood they can sense.
Foetal he goes, they stick the boot in, he goes tense.
One 'hero' aims a flying kick at the prone victim's head.
They continue, but he cares no more, for he's now dead.
The 'heroes' cheer and jeer, running off into the crowd.
Someone covers the body with a jacket, like a shroud.
The Sergeant walks up the mile long drive, to the bell.
Knowing what next will happen, knowing it will be Hell.
Flowers on the causeway, a sign of his life, now past.
Friends with shots, raise their glasses, "May his memory last!"

## A Fragile Jewel

I take up the fragile Jewel unsure.
My hands are ridiculous, rough cut, but clean,
Cleaned meticulously, for this sole purpose.
Testosterone fades as Oestrogen floods in.

I become a woman–man, as I gaze in raptures.
A giant would not dare try my hand.
At this very time I would gladly die!
My unending love pours forth.
I lay her once more down to sleep.
But slumber on knifes edge, aware.
Ready once more to be at her side.

## Pleiades Pilgrims

One day some strangers passed by this way,
They took stock of our planet, and laid down our DNA.
Then headed back to Pleiades, promising, one day, they'd return.
Leaving us to our own devices, to grow and to learn.
Watching from afar, and pledging no interference
We started to learn, alright, in the first instance.
Respecting our surroundings, the trees and the plants.
Also the animals, from the whales to the ants.
Then along came the industries, a desire to progress.
Mountains of refuse, creating a disgusting huge mess.
The waste became phenomenal, just a disgrace.
We've realised too late, with shame on our face.
That we've raped the earth, plundering our mother,
And stand toe to toe, now blaming each other.
We now have to face it, for out of time we have run.
As we move through the plane, our enemy the Sun.
Time waits for no one, and the ages have past.
The flares are upon us, we expect the big blast.
If by chance we survive, for it's not something we've earned.
Not realised the consequences, not anything we've learned.
Should the volcanoes die down, and flooding abate.
Could we all learn to love, instead of pure hate?
Cast out the money mongers, who seek, obeyance and control.
Build a charter of peace, and would everyone enrol?

I hope so, but fear, not, for there's so many who are blind.
They care just for themselves, and not for mankind.
Looking up to the stars, I let my mind wander.
Our family from the Pleiades, will they return I ponder.
With hope in my heart, I dream of the outcome we crave,
Our brothers and sisters to come back, for our souls to save.

## What a Difference the Day Makes

It was only two a.m., I went to bed with a good intention.
I would wake up early with a head full of invention.
Turning off the alarm at seven, "Just ten minutes more!"
At about nine thirty, I staggered through the lounge door.
"Tea! I think, and perhaps some golden toast"
"And while I'm waiting for the ping, I'll stick in a roast!"
Ten thirty now, as I finally sit down to write.
Turning on to 'Word' the page blank white.
Panic sets in as the brain goes into stall.
I know, promised to ring Nev, I'll give him a call!
Eleven thirty now, My word Nev sure can chat!
Oven buzzer going, S'pose I'd better see to that.
Twelve bells now, Better break for some lunch
The letter box clatters, The postman, I've a hunch.
Letters from the council, 'How we spend your money'.
What a pack of lies, you ain't fooling me sonny!
Statement from the bank, That's quite a blow,
Manager says come and see me, the old so and so.
Two thirty already? My how time flies.
Now knocking at the door my daughter, a lovely surprise!
Five o'clock now, "Are you stopping for tea?"
And as I bring in the roast, her face fills with glee.
Seven thirty now, as I open another bottle.
No, they're not bloodshot; it's more of a mottle.

Ten thirty now, as I say my last goodbye.
What a beautiful starry night, as I look to the sky
Finishing off the Merlot, as I sit before the screen.
Plonking wildly at the keyboard, words that can't be seen.
Keyboard must be broken; I'll turn it off for now.
Wake up at 10 a.m., wrong way round in bed, clueless how!
Sleeping on and off all day, waiting for the stillness.
Nothing to do with the wine must be some other illness!
Turning on the computer, it's only a half past one.
Love this wonderful quietness, I always get loads done!

## A Better Choice

There were crowds of people milling around.
A hundred voices, oh what a sound.
Chattering grownups, excited young.
Disable's wheelchairs, baby buggies among
The brightly coloured tables, goods stacked high.
"Don't give me ten pound, give me five!" The cry.
Stalls engorged with fruits, some exotic and rare.
Shiny red apple, Satsuma, melon and pear.
Child tugging at clothing, crying out for attention.
In his gaze, the next 'needed' invention.
Harassed housewife scuttles about with a purpose.
Bumped and barged, as she lets out the usual curses.
Young girls giggling at the young boys who follow.
They'll be walking hand in hand through the park tomorrow.
Husband and wife choosing a dress for her night out.
The tenth one tried, he's getting ready for the next bout.
Cushions and duvets, pictures, lampshades and throws.
Crocheted mittens and coats, and baby bonnets with bows.
Coffee, hotdogs, smothered in onions, what a glorious smell!
Bread, pastries and cakes, with warm doughnuts as well.

Malls and supermarkets are ok, they fulfil a purpose.
The variety and value, the choices they give us.
But when ease and cheapness is not always the target.
You just cannot compare to a good old Open Market.

## Just One More Dance

It was about six thirty that terrible morn.
A policeman had knocked bad news he had born.
An accident had occurred, not fatal, but bad.
We all felt the shock, when they said it was dad.
Mum was in tears, she bade us, "Please hurry!"
And as she sat there in silence, she shook, full of worry.
As we dashed into casualty, we were told "Please to wait!"
I could see mum breaking down and getting in a state.
Dad was in surgery, they told us at last.
This didn't bode well, it came like a blast.
Mum broke down completely, she now full of grief.
Try as we might, we could not raise her hopes or belief.
Sitting and waiting, minutes were as hours.
Mum seemed visibly to shrink, as we tried to be towers.
At last we were informed, immediate danger had passed.
Mum couldn't wait any longer; she would see him at last.
We visited for two weeks as dad regained strength.
And he was deemed to be able to return home at length.
Then horror of horrors, he took a turn for the worst.
Something inside had apparently burst.
Once more rushed in, to the hospital again.
He looked ashen grey and was in terrible pain.
He was snuffed out like a candle, we could not comprehend.
One minute he was with us and the next, was the end.
I had so much to say dad, I can't put it in short words.
It doesn't deserve just nouns, adjectives and verbs.
I just wish I could see you face to face, one more final chance.
To hug you close to me, say "I love you", watch you and mum dance.

Fred and Ginger you always would say, with pride and smiles.
To hear you sing 'Danny Boy', they would all travel miles.
You could hear a 'pin drop,' when you broke into song.
You were always the rock, always so strong.
I will never forget you, all the remainder of my days.
I will remember your silly phrases, and your funny old ways.
Mum's sadly, gone as well now, and I just wonder whether.
They have again found each other, once more together.
Gliding, arms around each other, toe to toe, head to head.
Dancing the time away in the beyond, like Ginger and Fred

## ?

Shards of glass exiting tear ducts,
A sharp bone, jammed in the gullet
Nausea flows in timely waves.
Hate and loneliness ride on the back of confusion.
The pain and self flagellation subsides.
Emptiness reigns supreme.
Trust erased from your personal dictionary.

## It's Just a Game!

She never got on with the 'Wembley look'
Somehow the hat, well it never quite stuck
To the top of her head, where it did clearly belong,
And as for the music! Call that a song?
She bade him "Goodbye!" midst the noise and tumult.
He'd complained to the ref, and called it "another bad result!"
Then came Rugby the mud, the tackling and the falls,
Men playing around with their odd shaped balls.
Huffing and puffing in a scrum with glee.
"Bathing in muddy water, with his mates, not me!"

Golf came next, that was never a blast,
Pulling his trolley, in the rain, coming last.
Then back to the "good old nineteenth!" the watering hole.
Telling all those 'hole-in-one' tales, selling one's soul,
"What a drive off the fifth, in one, on the green."
She'd scratched her head, must have been one, she hadn't seen!
She didn't explain, didn't want to, if he couldn't see.
She waited till the seventh, trolley in the lake, him on the tee!
"Cricket must be better!" she'd said in great hope.
Fast bowling, or nice slow balls, she reckoned she'd cope.
Infield and outfield and silly mid on.
Stopping for tea, delicious jam on a scone.
Rain stopped play, so all into the club.
To get your balls spinning, give it a good rub!
Wickets and bails, hard leather on the willow,
"Not again!" she cried, head stuck in her pillow.
"I know Tennis!" She'd give that a try.
"The ball was out, sir!" was the Umpire's cry.
Serving and volleys, give it plenty of top spin.
When it's over the line, argue like crazy, "It's in!"
Sat in the crowd, ball back and forth, head on a stick.
Making you dizzy and feeling really quite sick.
Thirty- forty, deuce, now break point you must get!
Drinks shortly after with the G and T set.
Floating about, out of depth, feeling like a prawn.
Too many G and T's, throwing- up on the lawn.
He suggesting she get a taxi handing her jacket.
Her shouting "Fine!" Belting him with his racket!
Tumbling out of the taxi, falling onto the floor.
A gentle hand lifting, it was John, "I'm from next door".
She looked up to his eyes, they were sparkling and blue.
Funny that, it had always been her favourite hue!
He smiled at her now, sending her in a tizzy.
Funny now she felt once again very dizzy.
He held her in strong arms, she felt safe and complete.
All that searching in vain, then the boy next door she'd meet.
No boots or pads no guards, bats, bullseye or double seven.
Just a man from next door, a bed, and her own games, just heaven!

## The Idol of Seth

But the call to do so was strong; he knew this was the only answer.
His mind made up, he would gather some supplies, so returned to his Stanza.
Fidor, his brave and trusty steed, instinctively knew, danger was afoot.
Avron knew this great animal would not fail, even if beaten, even if cut.
Bred for battle, his hide was scaly, armoured, coloured with green.
He would charge through the thickets, at great speed, hardly seen.
Avron went to Satia, he must tell her his plans, a way forward to freedom.
If this was not done, the enemy would swallow up their precious kingdom.
They had come, in hordes from the south, hearing of great wealth.
The goodly ones would do naught, so it was left to himself.
Forging forward he rode out, towards the wastelands, with the greatest of speed,
The great Fidor beneath him, a legend, renowned for his courage, a heroic steed.
Known for his fearlessness in the great battles of the slave wars of Tsor.
Battles so ferocious, thousands of Plaegians died, injured thousands more.
Most of their tribe had died, and all had seemed lost on that last fateful day.
When up stepped a man dressed in gold, holding aloft the idol, amidst the affray.
He spoke in a tongue, which was foreign to all who were there.
The battle faded to silence, as at him all did stare.
The light that shone forth was so fiercely powerful and so bright.
The men in the battle rubbed their eyes, supposing that it was night.
They rubbed and they blinked of their eyes but could see not a thing.
Confused and afraid, they crawled about, and then heard a voice ring.
"To take life and cause injury, will not be allowed, this has been decreed.
You were all put here, on this planet, for a purpose, you are all the seed.
Your violence will not be tolerated, your destruction will not occur.
For this crime, blind you will be, your penance, to remember how you were".

From that day till this in complete harmony, they'd lived out their days.
New born growing, taught by the old blind ones, learning their ways.
But now once again threatened by a force of evil and foul deed.
He rode out to meet them even though it had not been agreed.
Reaching the edge of the forest, and reigning Fidor to a halt,
He the great steed that he was, pawed the ground, eager for assault.
Avron waited and watched the trees for a noise or a sign.
Then suddenly they were their advancing, many in a line.
"Come no further, I warn you! Fore we wish you no ill!"
But sadly, he saw in their eyes, greed and readiness for the kill.
A voice from their leader boomed out from the ranks.
""No! I think we'll slaughter you slowly until you beg mercy, thanks!"
With that they moved forward with a chilling fierce cry.
So lifting up the idol, raising it aloft towards the sky.
He shielded his eyes and spoke out that dreadful phrase.
The words he'd heard from the goodly ones, and remembered all these days.
The light was as sunlight but burning and bright.
And instantly ten thousand men lost all their sight,
The Plaegians welcomed their blind adversaries, those who wanted to stay.
The others floundered homewards, to tell of that terrible day.
The statue was once more wrapped in the gold cloth from which it came.
And placed once again by the gravestone, of the man with no name.
They hoped the fable would spread far on whispered breath.
To hate and cause injury can bring a terrible fate, the wrath of Seth.

## A Bonding

He gave the order to move forward,
One colleague aft, one colleague starboard.
They moved with silent grace, speed and precision.
Like hungry wolves, senses alight, full of suspicion.
Rays of sunlight piercing dust and gloom.
Forming marbled walls around each room.
Their weapons held ready, in an arc like sweep.

Ready, to send the enemy ‘to sleep’.
They moved with purpose, as one machine.
The end would be swift, efficient and clean.
Having hunted them, for most of the day,
They now waited, all, longing for the affray.
An arm held out sideways, staying advance,
Signs for keep down, look, listen, take no chance.
Now moving slowly in silence, with purpose of deed.
The sniper moves forward to take up the lead.
They sit in the clearing, tired and at rest.
He looks around at his men, who’d given their best.
Smiling at them proudly, full of admiration, ten foot tall.
They’d broken the pain barriers; he felt bonds with them all.
The sniper took aim, making the shot deadly and clear,
He inched forward, on his stomach, his intent to get near.
The heat was intense, from his brow the sweat ran.
The other two flanked him now in a fan.
The explosions they started, a silent signal was given.
They moved forward, guns rattling, surprise element driven.
The group, who were sitting, looked around in surprise.
Shocked realisation on faces completed their demise.
The mission now complete, “Nice one lads!” came the call.
“That went quite smoothly, in fact, not difficult at all!”
“This calls for a celebration, perhaps a cold beer”
“No problem” said the paintballing adversaries, “we’ll get you next year!”

## Alone

He looked around him, the photographs, the music, his life.
He thought of the things that he’d done the good deeds and bad.
Remembering the help he’d given, in times of need, made him sad.
The promises they gave, the thanks, then let downs and betrayals.
He not wanting monetary reward, just the truth not denials.

They had taken so much from him, his life, night and day.
He'd been there for them all, knowing exactly what to say.
Now today, alone he stood, looking around at his lot.
No wife there to greet him, no happy kids had he got.
The one bedroom apartment, sounding hollow and cold.
She'd packaged up their life, taken off, house was sold.
"There's always someone else, we don't have a life,
I want a separation, I need space!" Said his wife.
He'd, gone on a bender, twice waking up in the gutters.
Turned off his phone, needing time, put up shutters.
Time heals they say, but believe, it leaves your soul with a scar.
Distance doesn't make a heart grow fonder; often it's a bridge too far.
Mustering strength from deep within, he pulled back from the abyss.
Vowing to collect his life together, even though them he did miss.
Then a knock on his door, steeling himself, he wouldn't send them away.
Opening it, he smiled, saying, "Hello, I'll be your councillor today"

## It's Not Rocket Science

As I stand in line amidst the buzzing supermarket throng,
A sign so large, in six inch red and white letters, hangs above.
**'Strictly, twelve articles maximum, make sure you belong.'**
A rotund woman in front of me, with her trolley gives a shove,
To the downtrodden chap in front of her, who turns and gives a grin.
She edges forward, to the head, oblivious to everyone about.
The cashier looks at her trolley with scorn, she sees the deadly sin.
'Scuze me Madam, have you not read the sign?" she let out a shout.
"But I've only got about twenty!" rotund let out a wail.
It was nearer to thirty, as she piled them on the belt.
As the assistant checked them through, she packed her bags like a snail.
And then when it came to paying, she fumbled and she felt,
In her pockets and her handbag, until her purse she eventually found.
Counted out her small change, only to find she hadn't it all.
Again checked her pockets, found change, dropping it to the ground.
Having counted and recounted it, "I'm ten pence short" came the call.

Fearing my life would end, before this woman was eventually sorted.
I slapped down ten pence, and smiled, saying "Have this one on me"

## She

She is beauty personified, wearing her heart on her sleeve,
Lighting up the room on entry, with her Joie de vivre.
Flits around the party, alighting on every man.
Each trying to capture her if they possibly can.
Giving each one just enough time, to flood mind and soul,
Then on to the next one, to enrapture every male her goal.
Like Hathor, she weaves and dances between them all.
Some women look and scowl, others think what gall.
Many just look on and smile, seeing she's no threat.
The men, eyes follow her, feeling just one regret,
That she did not stay longer to fill their hearts with joy.
Racking their brains 'til despair, for a plan they could employ,
To keep her lingering near them, so to drink in all her beauty.
She hovers once more, a moth drawn to the flame, in reality,
A butterfly so fragile, yet draws the breath of the strongest man.
Illusive, illuminated ,captivating, try catch her if you can.
None will imprison her, for she lives always to fly.
To clip her wings and deny her this she would only die.
Let her gossamer wings beat, and give her freedom's delight,
Then you may earn and feel her love one precious night

## An Expected Guest

He got up and gazed through the window once more,
Knowing that any moment her car would appear for sure.
She'd promised him faithfully he'd waited in all day.

Didn't give him a time, was busy, and so couldn't really say.
He sat down once more, wondering if the table he should lay.
Glancing at the card from Tom, 'Congrats sixty years young today!'
Remembering a time when he'd received a dozen not just one.
Special days of parties full of excitement and fun.
A horn sounded causing him to rise to take a look.
Just an impatient taxi driver, so in frustration, his fist he shook.
Where can she be? He thought, on his brow a worried frown.
She'd probably gone shopping, and it's busy in town.
He turned on the kettle once more, just of course, in case.
She'll knock on the door now, just watch this space!
Trying to read the paper once more, the same column six times.
Words having no meaning, they may as well have been just lines.
Opening the fridge checking he'd bought everything right.
All of her favourites were there, it was really quite a sight.
He turned on the television, then switched it off again.
Sat down, staring at the ceiling and noticed a stain.
Hearing a car engine he returned to the window to look out.
Seeing it was one of the neighbours he turned about,
And sat back down on the settee, once more picking up the paper.
She'd probably had to work over, so she'd come a bit later.
Laying the table, he got out the crockery, nothing less than his best .
After all she was his daughter, not some everyday guest.
Another car, but not her, he was now getting in a state.
He glanced at the clock again and realised it was now eight.
Putting away the crockery the table cloth, deciding this was bad.
She wouldn't be coming at all now, he thought, feeling sad.
Another hour passed, and he sighed, stood and looked about.
"Happy birthday mate, if she'd been less busy she'd have come without doubt!"

## A Soul In Torture

The sun sets sucking the daylight away,
As the moon rises triumphant, to see the demise of day.
A man hurries home collar turned against the chill.
Ignoring passersby, his mind set, determined will.
Shadows from the dark leap, coaxing, “come within!”
Grasping his coat front, tightening, fixed solemn grin.
Key duelling with the lock, as cold bit at gnarled fingers.
Hurriedly pushing into a dank dark hall he lingers.
Cold sweat beaded, now running down his furrowed brow.
Sliding to the red broken tiled hall below, he wonders how
He can cease his tormentor’s torturous whispers.
“Coward! You promised, just one more, I will not cease!”
He sits amongst friends, shadows in the dark, begging for peace.
“See you tomorrow guys” young Penny sings out loud.
Slipping down the lane, her route home away from the crowd.
Frosty breeze bites through hedges, grasping at her form.
Branches stroking and pulling, her coat now torn,
She stops, and examining, curses her bad luck.
No one saw or heard, as he, her young innocent form took.
Sitting in the dark weeping he wrings his red hands.
Whispering shadows around, plotting the morrow night’s plans.

## No One Was There

I went to the field where we'd played, no one was there.
The grass now long, where once it was bare.
A roundabout stood still, listing in its loneliness.
The awesome silence, a kind of plastic quietness.
I ambled down the lane, hawthorn overgrown.
Nettles lording over bluebells, hedgerows no more mown.
Our fortresses, a memory, jagged bricks protrude.
Fragments of the former thing to which it did elude.
I thought I heard laughter, for a moment, tho' not sure.
It sounded like a voice I'd heard so many years before.
In the distance I saw children playing in the wood.
Seeming so happy and carefree, I would've joined them if I could.
But the years have passed too many, since I frolicked without care.
All the faces came flooding back, almost more than I could bear.
Now walking up to the school gates, I heard the delicious din.
The memories of those rapturous years now came rushing in
To my mind, soaking it with joy and sadness, in the same degree.
I focussed as sharply as I was able, but my pals I couldn't see.
I strolled down to the sports fields now, and stood behind the goal.
Remembering all the games I'd played and I'd give my all, my soul,
Just to run the pitch one more time, and to be part of the team.
How long ago now was it? A hundred years since it did seem.
Yet, then again just yesterday, as a stood weeping through the stare.
I looked as far as I was able, but to my sadness, there was no one there.

## Waiting for No Man

It is something one cannot purchase, of that I'm sure,
But is something we all crave, and inevitably beg for more.
Not sustenance, nor is it food for the soul,
Neither something you can serve up, in a bowl.

Or quenching crystal clear water, from a babbling brook.
A kindly helping hand or friends to use as a crook.
We ignore it as it passes by, we rarely give a care.
Not realising we should take note and at least be aware.
Each cocks a snoot, and carries on, as if it doesn't matter.
Picking up precious moments, we them to the four winds scatter.
It's something we may wish for towards the end of our days,
Something we don't understand , its speed never ceases to amaze.
I'm just grateful that I've had, and embraced most of mine.
The currency we all spend so quickly, what I speak of, is time.

## That Time of Year

Driven white snow crunching under foot,
Setting out for the annual trip, making sure the door's shut.
Behind you delighted children laughing wildly.
Decorating the tree, mum accepting the distraction gladly.
Delicious scents of Cinnamon, apple and spices,
Chocolate Santas, sweets and Candied fruit slices.
Reaching the Butchers, you take in the sight.
Freshly plucked foul, honey roast hams glistening in the light.
Next to the Off-license, buying Port, Liquors and Beer.
To sup with your family and friends with good cheer.
It's that time of year once more again to rejoice.
To join with your relatives, to give thanks in good voice.
It's a time to remember all those you left behind this year.
To remember them with joy and love and perhaps yes a tear.
But as you return home at last through the crowds and melee.
The kids all shout with excitement and obvious glee.
Glad to see your return, with fascination and delight.

Trying to glimpse those presents you'll be wrapping tonight,
The final chore, the wrapping, something you dread.
You pour out a drink, for yourself and the love of your life.
And then struggle with the paper and tape which causes you strife.
Finally to your relief now, she takes charge of the event.
So you give her a kiss saying, "My love you're heaven sent".
Finally now relaxed, you sink down into the sofa.
Glad at last, that the hassle and tussling is over.
You look at each other, with that understanding smile.
Gazing at the tree, presents underneath it in a pile.
Although it's memorable and exciting, and without price.
It comes and goes quickly, and seems over in a trice.
Still Christmas is the best time, and we must try enjoying it with cheer.
And pray hope that we will all be here to enjoy it next year.

www.ingramcontent.com/pod-product-compliance
Ingram Content Group UK Ltd.
Pitfield, Milton Keynes, MK11 3LW, UK
UKHW020227250726
13967UKWH00001B/232

9 781446 776728